WORK IT, GIRL

OPRAH WINFREY

WORK IT, GIRL

RUN THE SHOW LIKE CEO
OPRAH
WINFREY

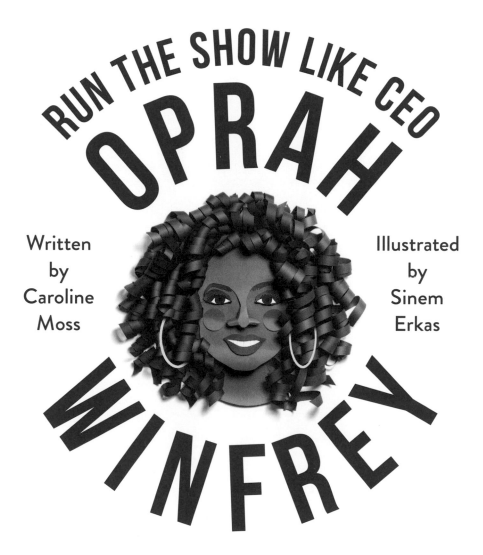

Written
by
Caroline
Moss

Illustrated
by
Sinem
Erkas

Frances Lincoln
Children's Books

Chapter 1

Oprah's Early Childhood: The Little Preacher

Oprah Winfrey sat on the steps outside her grandmother's farmhouse in Kosciusko, Mississippi, inspecting the dress she had been given to wear that morning. She was only four years old, not even old enough to go to school, but she knew she was different than the other children she would see in town and at church.

While other girls wore pretty cotton dresses in hues of blue or yellow or pink, Oprah's dress was made out of a potato sack. Her grandmother, Hattie Mae Lee, had fashioned it for her. They were very poor, and at $2.50, pretty dresses were too expensive for Hattie Mae to buy. Hattie Mae, like Oprah, was black, and in the 1950s, being a black woman in the South meant you didn't have a lot of opportunities to get good jobs that paid good money. It also meant that white people treated you differently, like you were less worthy of a good life because of the color of your skin. And so, Oprah was made fun of by other kids for being a poor black girl who wore potato sack dresses. They called her "sack girl."

Oprah clutched her corncob doll tightly and thought about her mother, Vernita Lee. She hadn't seen her mother for a few years. Vernita had been a teenager when she had Oprah on 29th January, 1954, and she didn't have a job to support herself or her daughter. She went north to find work as a maid, but she couldn't bring Oprah with her. So, Oprah lived with Hattie Mae on the farm.

Oprah knew life was harder for her because of the color of her skin. Her grandmother was born in 1900, a revolutionary time for black people in America. Slavery had been abolished but segregation and discrimination were still deep-rooted in the country, especially in the South. Though Hattie Mae was not born a slave, she was often treated like a lesser human by the white people she worked for. And yet, Hattie Mae would tell Oprah that she should hope to grow up to work for some "good white folks" who would sometimes spare her

IT WAS HARD TO MAKE FRIENDS WHEN YOU WERE "SACK GIRL."

leftovers from their dinner table. It seems like an awful thing to say to a little girl now, but remember that back then, this paltry offering of food to a woman who worked long hours for you and your family was seen as a radical act of kindness from a white person to a black person. Hattie Mae could not imagine a world where she might hope to be treated any better, and so she couldn't imagine one for Oprah either.

"I REGRET MY GRANDMOTHER DID NOT LIVE TO SEE I'VE GOT SOME GOOD WHITE FOLKS WORKING FOR ME," OPRAH WOULD SAY, DECADES LATER.

That child is gifted!

Oprah watched a cockroach run back and forth across the stoop and wondered how long it would be until Hattie Mae would finish washing the white people's clothes in the basin of hot water and help Oprah with her reading and writing. Oprah loved reading and writing and Hattie Mae thought Oprah was a wonderful reader and writer. But more than that, Oprah loved to talk. She could talk all day, and never tire of it. Every Sunday, Hattie Mae would take Oprah to church. While other children Oprah's age would fuss around and get antsy, Oprah listened intently to the words being spoken. Soon, she was asked to recite verses in front of the whole congregation!

She was never nervous. She loved that everyone was listening to what she had to say. It made her feel special; like she was a voice worth listening to.

"Hattie Mae," the old ladies at church would say, "that child is gifted!"

Other kids might have called her "sack girl" but the church congregation started to call her "the little preacher."

And Oprah, even though she was only four, knew she wanted to grow up and get paid to talk.

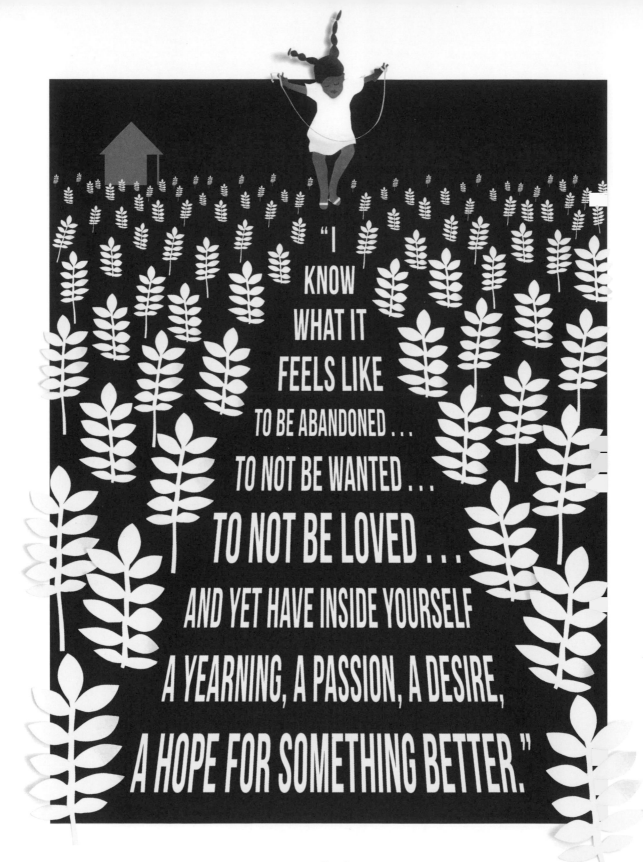

"I KNOW WHAT IT FEELS LIKE TO BE ABANDONED ... TO NOT BE WANTED ... TO NOT BE LOVED ... AND YET HAVE INSIDE YOURSELF A YEARNING, A PASSION, A DESIRE, A HOPE FOR SOMETHING BETTER."

— Oprah

"I REMEMBER A SPECIFIC MOMENT, WATCHING MY GRANDMOTHER HANG THE CLOTHES ON THE LINE, AND HER SAYING TO ME, 'YOU ARE GOING TO HAVE TO LEARN TO DO THIS,' AND ME BEING IN THAT SPACE OF AWARENESS AND KNOWING THAT MY LIFE WOULD NOT BE THE SAME AS MY GRANDMOTHER'S LIFE."

— Oprah

Chapter 2

Growing Up

Life with Hattie Mae, even though they didn't have any money, was good for Oprah. Hattie Mae was supportive and loving. She encouraged her granddaughter to do her very best. She provided structure and routine to Oprah's life, which is important when you are a kid, and especially important when you have goals and dreams like Oprah did. When it came to reading and writing, Oprah flourished so much she was able to skip ahead a grade! The future was looking bright.

But when Oprah was six, Hattie Mae became ill and could no longer take care of her granddaughter. Oprah had to move north to Milwaukee and live with her mother, who had taken work as a maid.

In the time since her mother had left, she had given birth to another daughter named Patricia, who she seemed to love more than she loved Oprah.

When Oprah arrived at the Milwaukee boarding house where her mother lived, she felt alone and abandoned. The house was rundown and unfamiliar. It was cold. Oprah missed Hattie Mae terribly. She barely knew her mother! She wanted to return to her grandmother, to the farm. She would even wear a sack dress if it meant she could go back home.

Six-year-old Oprah tried to reason with herself. After all, she thought, at least she had a place to sleep. Many people didn't have a place to sleep.

But then came an unimaginable turn of events. On her first night at the boarding house, Oprah was told she was not allowed to sleep inside because her skin was too dark. Her half-sister, Patricia, had much lighter skin, and so she was afforded the comfort of a roof over her head. But six-year-old Oprah was sent to sleep outside on the porch, alone.

Oprah tried really hard to make the best of her time with her mother, but it wasn't the same as being with Hattie Mae. Vernita hardly knew her daughter, having left her behind at such a young age. And Vernita was working long, exhausting hours without much pay. Vernita didn't have time to spend with Oprah on reading and writing like Hattie Mae did, and

she didn't much care that her daughter seemed to have a special gift. There would be no more preaching at church, and no more impressing the older ladies in the front row who called her "the little preacher."

Instead, Oprah found herself in terrible situations. The people in her life, both family members and friends of her family, were not nice to Oprah. They abused her and treated her horribly. Oprah felt so alone. She had a hard time concentrating on the things that used to make her happy back on the farm with Hattie Mae.

SHE HAD TO HOLD ON TO THE HOPE THAT ONE DAY, THINGS WOULD GET BETTER.

Soon, Vernita grew impatient with trying to raise two daughters and work long hours cleaning houses. Oprah's prayers were about to be answered! She was temporarily sent to live with her father, Vernon. He was much more supportive of Oprah, and had more time for her. He encouraged her growth in reading and writing and speaking, and he was strict—in a good way. But it wouldn't last for long.

Back and forth, back and forth. Oprah was shuttled between Vernon and Vernita for nearly a decade. She craved stability, craved just one place she could call "home".

Oprah then began her high school education under Vernita's parenting in Milwaukee, but was constantly getting into trouble. Most teenagers argue with their parents, but Oprah and Vernita took arguing to a new level. Oprah had even figured out how to steal money from her mother so she could try to imitate the lifestyles of the richer girls at school. She was still made fun of for being poor, and she would do anything to make the name-calling and harassment end, even if she knew deep down that stealing was wrong.

Soon, Vernita threw up her hands and sent 14-year-old Oprah back to live with her father permanently in Tennessee.

Chapter 3

A Bright Future Ahead

High school under the guidance of her father proved to be just what Oprah needed. He was strict, which was good. He made sure she got good grades, and that she wasn't letting drama with friends or with boys get in the way of her studies. He even made Oprah read one book a week—separate from her school assignments—and write a report on it. That was strict! But it helped Oprah become an even stronger reader and writer, and maybe most importantly, a more independent thinker.

It was at this point that Oprah read

a book that would change her outlook on life. Maya Angelou's autobiography, *I Know Why The Caged Bird Sings*, spoke to Oprah, and the theme of a young black girl's experience growing up in America was like a mirror reflecting back on her teenage self. This book came to her at a time when she saw very little representation of black women in positions of power, of education, and of respect. Maya's message was proof that Oprah's big dreams were not silly or a waste of time; that they could truly be a reality if she believed in their power. So 16-year-old Oprah made a big decision.

"I AM GOING TO GO FOR MY DREAMS," SHE THOUGHT, "AND NO ONE WILL GET IN MY WAY."

Oprah thought about all of the things she was really good at—reading, public speaking, writing, and of course, being part of the drama and debate teams at school. Then she thought about which of those things she really loved. The answer was obvious: Public speaking. Remember when Oprah was little and she would go to church to captivate audiences of adults and children alike? Remember the little old ladies in church who would say, "Hattie Mae, that child is gifted!"? Oprah wondered if that was still true more than 10 years later. So, she entered a speaking competition.

Oprah wasn't nervous when it was her turn to speak at the competition. She felt at home when she was talking in front of crowds. She knew she was writing her own future by listening to the voice deep down inside of her guiding her towards what she would later call her "truth."

Oprah won the speaking competition, and the grand prize: a four-year scholarship to the University of Tennessee. This was a huge opportunity for Oprah. College was expensive, and up until she won the scholarship, she didn't know how she was going to pay for it.

She thought about Hattie Mae, and how she had only wanted Oprah to live up to her highest potential. There are lots of ways to become successful, and they don't always involve college. But college was a dream of Oprah's, and before she won the competition, she thought it was a dream that would never come true. But now it was actually happening! Oprah had secured the ticket to her very bright future.

Chapter 4

The First Black News Anchor in Nashville

Oprah really loved going to college at the University of Tennessee. She made lots of friends, and professors and peers alike knew Oprah was very smart and had a bright future ahead of her.

At the end of high school, Oprah started working at WVOL, a local black radio station, where the managers and producers liked her so much that they asked her to continue to work for them during her time at the University of Tennessee. This was a big deal. Usually college students are not old enough or experienced enough to work professional jobs until they graduate with a degree in order to be qualified. But as we already know, many adults saw potential in Oprah, just like her grandmother Hattie Mae did.

Having the job at WVOL helped Oprah get her name out into the world and soon, another opportunity presented itself in Nashville. This time, a TV station wanted to hire Oprah to read the headlines on the nightly news. She would be the first black news anchor in Nashville on WLAC-TV. Oprah was only in her early twenties and she was already making history.

But she wouldn't stop there.

Oprah's star was on the rise. While she was still in college, a news channel in Baltimore contacted her with a job offer. She didn't know what to do. Should she stay in college and get her degree? Probably, Oprah thought. Or maybe she should leave for the job. Oprah asked herself: Don't folks go to college so they can get jobs? And now she was getting a job—a good job! It was just in a different timeline than expected, and so she didn't know if it was right.

Oprah decided it was okay to do things out of the expected order sometimes. One of her professors encouraged her to take the job in Baltimore, which really helped Oprah feel like she was making the right choice for herself. She had wondered how she'd fit in biology class with her job, but her professor laughed at her worries.

"THAT'S WHY YOU GO TO SCHOOL, FOOL!" HE TOLD OPRAH.

So Oprah went to Baltimore, thinking she had made it—that all of her dreams had come true. Everything was going to be great ...

"
LUCK IS A MATTER OF PREPARATION MEETING OPPORTUNITY
"
—Seneca

Chapter 5

Trouble in Baltimore

Baltimore was supposed to be Oprah's Big Break. To her, this job as a co-host on a news show meant all of her dreams were coming true. She had come from an impoverished upbringing and was now breaking barriers Hattie Mae could have only dreamed about Oprah breaking. Oprah had made it. She had reached the top!

Not so fast. Baltimore was not as welcoming a place to Oprah as Nashville had been and it started to make Oprah nervous. She'd never had trouble making friends before, but now she was having a difficult time finding people who really understood her. Her new company didn't understand her either. Before Oprah started her new job, her bosses were trying to come up with a catchy way to get people talking about the show.

They came up with an idea. The question, "What is an Oprah?" was plastered on billboards and buses all over the city. No one knew the answer and it got the city talking. "Do you know what an Oprah is?" people would ask their friends. No one knew. How could they find out? By watching the show.

Looking back on this, it is easy to understand why this kind of question is not appropriate! It tells people that this name is so different, so wild and unheard of, that it could not possibly belong to a human. An "Oprah" is just so crazy and wacky and silly, instead of it just being a name you might have never heard before. "What is an Oprah?" was a bad idea.

Oprah later said she felt like she didn't live up to the hype of the marketing campaign.

There was one silver lining for Oprah in Baltimore: meeting Gayle King, a woman who would soon become her very best friend. Almost everything else was a nightmare.

"PEOPLE WERE EXPECTING THIS BIG SOMETHING," SHE SAID. THE BUILD-UP WAS SO STRONG. AND I'M JUST A COLORED GIRL WITH A LOT OF HAIR … AND EVERYBODY'S LIKE, 'WHAT? THAT'S WHAT AN OPRAH IS? SHE'S NOT ALL THAT!'"

Oprah's co-host, a man named Jerry Turner, did not like her and he did not try to hide it. Just like being a good friend, being a good colleague means you support the people you work with, and you help them to do their best so that you can do your best. Jerry Turner did not do this for Oprah, because he did not want a co-host at all. He wanted the whole show to himself. And he let the big bosses at the Baltimore station know it.

"Every chance he got he would embarrass me," Oprah recalled.

Oprah would sometimes get emotional reading the news, which Turner hated. He thought it was unprofessional. The producers didn't necessarily disagree. Once, when reporting a story about a house fire, Oprah brought the displaced family warm blankets. She was later scolded for "involving herself in the story." Her bosses wanted her to be a journalist and remain neutral and uninvolved. But being a journalist wasn't what Oprah wanted, she started to realize. She didn't want to just report the news, even though that meant she got to be "paid to talk." She liked meeting people and hearing their stories and helping them. Like the family who survived their house fire: These were people in need, regardless of what her job was. Why shouldn't she be trying to help them? Oprah's do-gooder attitude just made Jerry Turner dislike her more.

The bosses at Baltimore knew things weren't going well between Jerry and Oprah, and they were left with a choice: They could either choose Jerry, who was their long-time star, or they could choose Oprah, who was brand new and still getting used to the job. Who do you think they chose?

If you guessed Jerry Turner, you were right.

Oprah was called into her boss's office on April 1st, 1977 and was told she

ALL OF A SUDDEN OPRAH WENT FROM LIVING HER DREAM OF "GETTING PAID TO TALK" TO DOING ODDS AND ENDS AROUND THE PRODUCTION STUDIO.

would be transferred to a job where she was almost never on camera. This was a demotion, but her bosses made it sound like a great opportunity. Oprah thought they were pranking her with an April Fool's Day joke, until she realized they were serious. She was so humiliated, but she had to go along with the changes for fear of being fired. She didn't have another job waiting for her, so if she had quit, she'd have been out of money and with no way to pay her rent or bills. It was such a hard position to be in.

"DON'T FIGHT THEM. JUST FIND A NEW WAY TO STAND."

— Oprah

Chapter 6

People Are Talking

Oprah wouldn't be on the bottom for long. There was another person at the Baltimore station who really liked her and saw a lot of promise. His name was Richard Sher, and in 1978 he and Oprah launched a talk show called *People Are Talking* at the same station that had demoted Oprah down the ladder just a year earlier.

Critics were not convinced, but it didn't matter because viewers loved their chemistry. Now Oprah had Gayle, Richard Sher (and her own drawer full of cookies in his kitchen!), and her *People Are Talking* producer Arlene Weiner on her side. She had finally made some friends and was starting to find her community.

THIS WAS BIG. Having a producer as a friend was a favorable position to be in; after all, this is what helped give Jerry Turner the edge to push Oprah out years earlier. But Oprah didn't use her relationship with Arlene to lord over anyone else. Instead, she saw Arlene as a mentor, and someone to look up to.

Arlene also had a lot of money, and Oprah didn't know anyone who had a lot of money. When she would go over to Arlene's house for dinner or coffee, she would look out into the backyard and count the trees on Arlene's property.

"THAT BECAME MY STANDARD: 'I'M GONNA HAVE ME A HOUSE ONE DAY WITH SIX TREES,'" OPRAH SAID.

"I determined then that's what really rich is: Being able to have six trees in your yard."

Things were getting better for Oprah in Baltimore. She realized then that there was never going to be a finale to her career, that there would always be ups and downs. And at the moment, her rollercoaster was going up, up, up. She heard there was a morning show in Chicago looking for a host, and Oprah thought it might be time again to take another leap of faith.

A.M. Chicago wanted people to send in audition tapes, and there was a tight deadline. Oprah would have to make sure she sent in her tape on time. She wasn't sure if it was going to get done, and she was really nervous she might miss her chance.

At the last minute, Oprah submitted her tape. She hoped it wasn't too late, but she wouldn't know for sure for a few weeks. She was certain there was a lot of competition and Oprah was not convinced she would beat out everyone else who wanted the job.

Meanwhile, in Chicago, a man named Dennis Swanson popped a tape into his machine, from a woman named Oprah Winfrey who was working down in Baltimore in a newsroom. He saw her cheerful disposition and heard her enthusiastic voice and decided she was right for the job. He thought Oprah had a spark he hadn't seen from watching any of the other tapes. He wanted to know more about Oprah. Maybe she was what *A.M. Chicago* was missing.

Back in Baltimore, things were still going well for Oprah. She had Gayle, her BFF, and she was having fun at work with Arlene. Part of her was hoping she would hear back from someone at *A.M. Chicago* but another part of her was thinking, Well, this job feels pretty safe. I don't really want to take another risk anytime soon. Even though it was a few years earlier, the memory of her big "failure" co-hosting with Jerry Turner made her nervous about taking yet another new job in a new city. What if she failed again? What if she couldn't find a friend in the newsroom, or worse, what if people made fun of her name again?

Maybe it would be a good thing if she didn't get the job.

Then the phone rang. It was Dennis Swanson. He told Oprah he thought she was going to be a big star in Chicago. Oprah had butterflies in her stomach but they were excited butterflies. She decided to take a leap of faith, and moved up to Chicago to host their morning talk show.

Unlike her other jobs where she read headlines and talked about the news, *A.M. Chicago* was more fun, but it left more room for error. Guests came on to teach Oprah how to cook a specific dish —

BUT HER MISTAKES ONLY MADE HER AUDIENCE LOVE HER MORE.

Oprah didn't cook at all.

She was humble, she was funny, and viewers loved funny. They craved funny. They weren't getting funny from any other morning show.

And Oprah was happy! Unlike being in Baltimore, which always felt a

little foreign to Oprah, Chicago truly felt like home. In fact, Oprah always felt an overwhelming sense of belonging whenever she'd fly somewhere else and then come back to Chicago. She would see the skyline of the city and feel like it was where she was meant to be. That was important to Oprah, and it reflected in her work at the TV show.

Within a month, *A.M. Chicago* ratings had skyrocketed to the top! Everyone was watching—and loving—

Oprah. She was even in a movie: Steven Spielberg's "The Color Purple", and she was nominated for an Academy Award. She was becoming a star, just like Dennis Swanson said she would be.

WHICH GAVE THE PRODUCERS AN IDEA ...

"TURN YOUR WOUNDS INTO WISDOM."

— Oprah

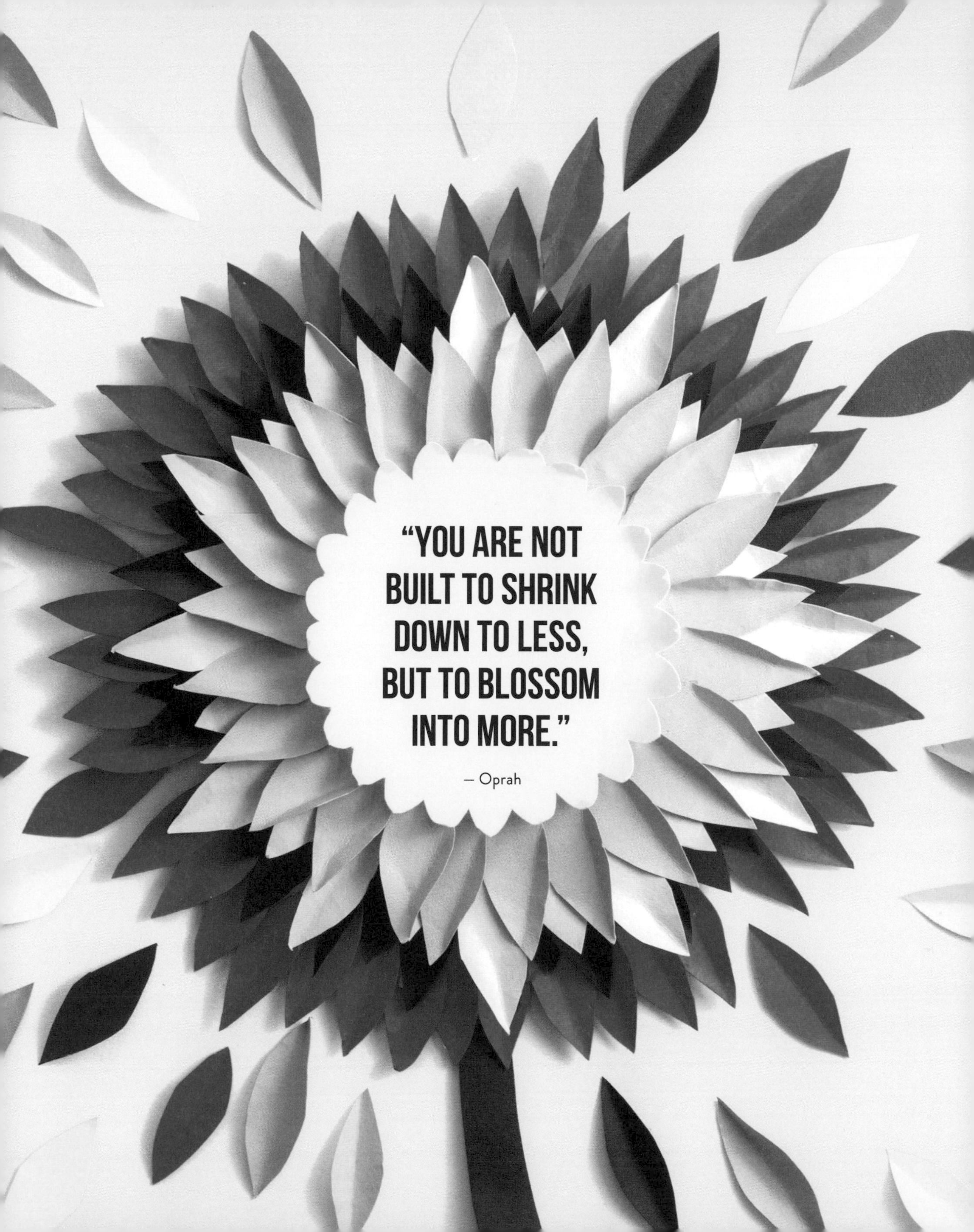

"YOU ARE NOT
BUILT TO SHRINK
DOWN TO LESS,
BUT TO BLOSSOM
INTO MORE."

— Oprah

Chapter 7

The Oprah Winfrey Show

A.M. Chicago became *The Oprah Winfrey Show* in September 1986. Now everyone in the country could watch Oprah if they wanted to!

Was this it? This time it was undeniable: Oprah was finally, really and truly, being paid to talk, as she had declared she would when she was a little girl, to her grandmother Hattie Mae. But the pressure was also on. Chicago already loved her. What about the rest of America?

Oprah knew she only had a short amount of time to convince people her show was worth watching. She had to think BIG.

At first, she thought she would need a big famous name to help draw people in to watching her, but Oprah couldn't convince a celebrity to come on the show. They didn't know who she was, and they didn't care. She would send celebrities gifts like mink teddy bears, hoping that would make them want to come and talk to her, but it didn't work. She needed another plan, or she was going to crash and burn before she even got a chance to show the world what she could do!

She had to come up with another way to get the audience excited. People like talking to their friends, she thought, so what if she became the audience's friend? She needed to talk to them like she was in their living room discussing the things women cared about, the same things Oprah and Gayle cared about!

How do you make a friend? Sometimes it happens when you let your guard down in front of other people and show them that you are a regular human being. So, the cameras turned on Oprah on the very first episode of her show and Oprah, who was nervous, blurted:

"I HAVE HIVES UNDER MY ARMPITS!" — RIGHT OUT TO THE WHOLE WORLD.

The audience laughed and laughed and laughed. They weren't making fun of her. They weren't thinking, "What is an Oprah?" They were relating to her! This was any TV host's dream. Oprah was delighted. The producers were delighted.

And the viewers kept coming back for more. Oprah was like a friend that everyone wanted to sit with at lunch—not because they wore the best clothes or had

the most money—but because she was a good listener, a good speaker, and helped you understand, learn, and care about things.

America had been looking for a friend like Oprah Winfrey.

But she was still new on the job, and had a lot to learn.

As a child, Oprah famously said she wanted to be paid to talk, but what does that mean? Does it mean you just get to go in front of an audience and talk about whatever you want, and whatever you think, and since you have the microphone you automatically get to be right? Some people out there might say yes! But not Oprah. She knew the real secret of having a talk show: Listening. She listened to her friends and her viewers. She listened to the people who worked with her. She even listened to people who didn't agree with her, like people who believed she wasn't worthy of her success because she was black, or because she was a woman.

Instead of saying, "I don't care what you say, it's my show," Oprah started inviting people with different views to come and talk to her, which helped people at home have those same conversations with their families and friends.

All of a sudden, everyone at home was watching Oprah, and not just watching the fun shows about makeovers and weddings and exercising. They were learning new perspectives on topics like race and gender and politics.

Oprah Winfrey, the person who used to cry while reading the headlines in Baltimore, who was humiliated because another colleague wanted the spotlight all to himself, and who wasn't totally sure if leaving Baltimore for Chicago was a good choice, was now captivating viewers across the country. It was her empathy and understanding of humans that pulled them in.

Her rollercoaster was still climbing up, up, up.

WHO ARE GOING TO TAKE YOU HIGHER."

— Oprah

Chapter 8

Staying Humble

By the 1990s, Oprah was a true celebrity. Remember when celebrities didn't want to come and talk to Oprah because they didn't know who she was? Suddenly, everyone wanted to come on Oprah's show because they knew everyone at home was watching her on television. She was getting so famous that she started her own production company called Harpo Studios. (Hint: Write Oprah backwards—what does that spell … ?)

Publicists were begging for their clients—celebrities, authors, politicians, even famous pets—to get a chance to be on her show. She was the most popular ticket in town. Once, the most famous actor at the time—Tom Cruise—jumped up and down on Oprah's couch during the show! President Obama and Michelle Obama even came to talk to her. You couldn't imagine that happening when Oprah first started, and neither could she.

If she had wanted to, Oprah could have said, "I don't want to talk to any regular people anymore. I just want famous people to come on my show." Her popularity and wealth could have easily made Oprah forget about her humble beginnings, but Oprah knew that it was actually the regular people like you and me that her audience loved hearing about and listening to the most. That was why they wanted to watch her show every day. It was fun to see celebrities, too, of course, but you could see celebrities on any television show. You could only see Oprah on one—*The Oprah Winfrey Show.*

She was a household name, but Oprah knew a little something about being a good colleague and friend to those who had helped her reach success. Remember Dennis Swanson, who saw Oprah's *A.M. Chicago* audition tape and hired her? Oprah still talks about him, and credits him for her success even though it's been over 30 years. He was the first person Oprah mentioned in her acceptance speech at the Golden Globes.

Oprah is the most famous and influential business woman in the world, but she is always giving credit and thanks to others who came before her. What kind of a person does that make her? Being humble and having humility makes people like you, even as you become rich and famous. Oprah never forgets "the little people" but more importantly, she never thinks of anyone as "little people" to begin with.

To stay grounded through her meteoric rise to celebrity, Oprah kept a framed photo of her grandmother, Hattie Mae, on her desk.

The photo is the only one Oprah has of her grandmother, and she is wearing her maid's uniform. Oprah says that photo reminds her that she is the dream of her grandmother, who probably could never have imagined a future this bright for the young toddler who used to captivate churches.

But Oprah wanted to do more. She thought about Hattie Mae and the chances she never got. She thought about her mother, working long hours cleaning

houses and being discriminated against for the color of her skin. She thought about her father, who helped give her the structure she needed to achieve her dreams when she was a high school and college student. She thought about herself as a young girl with big dreams, hoping someone, somewhere, someday would give her an opportunity to shine. She had gotten that opportunity and now she wanted to make sure others like her got that opportunity, too.

SHE WANTED TO GIVE BACK.

Chapter 9

Oprah's Intention

B y the new millennium Oprah wasn't just everyone's favorite talk show host—she was everyone's favorite celebrity.

People trusted her. People wanted to be like her, or be her best friend. And Oprah had a way of making you feel like if she met you, she might want to be your best friend, too ... even through a television! That's magical.

So Oprah started a book club, where she recommended her favorite titles that you could go buy in the store, and each book would have a little sticker on it to say it was Oprah's favorite. If your book was selected by Oprah, you could bet that your book would be a huge success.

People marveled at her ability to sell a book, and that made them think.

If Oprah can make someone drive to the bookstore and spend $20 on a book because she said it's good, what else could Oprah get people to buy? They started sending Oprah products. Hundreds and hundreds and hundreds of products. Sweaters and refrigerators and snow boots and even brownies! Stores sent jewelry and expensive purses and cameras and even a panini maker. Oprah started picking out the products she liked the most, and every Thanksgiving she'd dedicate a whole episode to telling the audiences at home about her "Favorite Things", ahead of holiday shopping.

But Oprah wanted to step it up.

She started shifting her focus for the show around this time. Now it was less about "living your best life" and more about setting your intention. What does that mean? For Oprah, it meant asking, "Why are we doing this?" for everything she and her producers chose to do on the show. It wasn't enough to answer, "Well it would be fun!" or "Because people will love it." There had to be a deeper meaning, or intention, behind everything Oprah did on and off the show.

She decided that everyone who went to the live taping of her "Favorite Things" episode would get to take home every single product for free. She chose those audiences very carefully. One year, the audience was full of public school teachers who thought they were there for a show about education. But then faint jingle bells would start to ring out, and everyone at home would get to watch everyone's shock as the audience screamed and jumped up and down when Oprah would announce that they were there for "FAVOOORITE THINGS!"

The intention behind this was being able to make sure all of these free gifts were going home with people who truly deserved to have them.

But Oprah always wanted to do more. She had an idea to give away 11 cars to people who really needed cars. Wow! But it still wasn't enough. What if she could give away a car to every single person in the audience?

Producers of the show remember working really hard to help Oprah's visions come true. They sent out a survey to people who wanted to sit in the audience to see if they could learn more about how they got to work, or what they needed.

Eventually, they put together an audience of hundreds of people who had said a new car would change their lives for the better. And gave them all a set of keys to brand new cars!

OPRAH CARED ABOUT HER FANS AND VIEWERS SO MUCH.

Oprah was so happy doing *The Oprah Winfrey Show*. She got to help people, meet people, and, of course, she was getting paid to talk. What could be better?

For years, Oprah starred on her own show. But she was also doing a ton of work behind-the-scenes. She was committed to changing the world, and she knew that talking about changing the world was only one part of the bigger picture. All of a sudden, Oprah was the world's most powerful – and richest – African-American woman. But that kind of visibility and power came with responsibility to do good. She started the *Oprah's Angel Network* where she gave lots of money towards helping underprivileged kids get better, richer, fuller educations. She was named one of the most influential women, and one of the most generous.

Chapter 10

Giving Back

Oprah could not keep up the pace of her professional life forever. In 2010, she felt that it was time to say goodbye to *The Oprah Winfrey Show.* A voice deep inside of her told her that she had done everything she could on the show and it was time to leave. People were sad, and so many tried to convince her to stay on the air forever, but Oprah did what she did best—she listened to herself. She knew people felt like Oprah was leaving them.

But of course, she would never be truly out of the picture. Oprah was already an icon all over the world. Though she created a production company to help give others a voice and a platform in her absence, she remained steadfast in her decision that there would be no more *Oprah Winfrey Show.* It was a difficult decision, but ultimately, a necessary one.

For the show's finale, Oprah's top producer, Sherri Salata, planned major surprises. It was a lot of work to surprise Oprah, because she was so involved in everything the show did. But Sherri convinced Oprah to leave the finale shows alone so the producers could plan something really big. Boy, was Oprah shocked. The finale was taped in a big stadium in Chicago, and all of her celebrity friends came to say goodbye and wish her well. Remember when Oprah couldn't convince any celebrities to join the show? Things had definitely changed! It wasn't the celebrities that made the finale so special to Oprah, however, even though it was fun to see her friends. The most touching moment of all was when 400 Morehouse College graduates walked on stage. These 400 men had their college educations funded by Oprah. She stepped in because none of these boys would have been able to afford to go to

college. Now they came back to thank her, and walked on stage as Kristin Chenowith sang "For Good" from her Broadway show, *Wicked*.

Oprah started to cry with happiness, just like producers knew she would. The audience was crying too. It was the perfect ending to the show and the perfect beginning to a life full of giving back even more.

Since leaving *The Oprah Winfrey Show*, Oprah has stayed in the public eye as a force for good. She is no longer being paid to talk, technically, but she doesn't

need to. Now, she travels the globe as a beacon of hope and inspiration to so many. People really listen to what she has to say, perhaps because she spent so much time really listening to others. She has written books, performed in movies, and made education a priority.

In January 2018, Oprah was awarded the Cecil De Mille award for lifetime achievement at the Golden Globes, and her speech drew a standing ovation as well as millions of views on the internet.

One of the things she said really stuck ...

"I'VE INTERVIEWED AND PORTRAYED PEOPLE WHO'VE WITHSTOOD SOME OF THE UGLIEST THINGS LIFE CAN THROW AT YOU, BUT THE ONE QUALITY ALL OF THEM SEEM TO SHARE IS AN ABILITY TO MAINTAIN HOPE FOR A BRIGHTER MORNING, EVEN DURING OUR DARKEST NIGHTS. SO I WANT ALL THE GIRLS WATCHING HERE, NOW, TO KNOW THAT A NEW DAY IS ON THE HORIZON! AND WHEN THAT NEW DAY FINALLY DAWNS, IT WILL BE BECAUSE OF A LOT OF MAGNIFICENT WOMEN ..."

— Oprah

In making that speech, it felt as if Oprah was handing off her brightly burning torch to a world of little girls with dreams of becoming the next powerful public figure.

When Oprah was a little girl, Hattie Mae hoped her granddaughter would have a life full of opportunities she could only dream about. Now, Oprah is wishing all of those same dreams for you.

Learn to run the show like Oprah!

10 key lessons from Oprah's life

1 **Learn from the people in your life who love you!**
Hattie Mae was Oprah's biggest fan and her greatest
teacher. Though she was much older than Oprah, she had
life experience that helped light the way for Oprah's future.
Hattie Mae's life gave Oprah perspective. There are many
people in your life who have different perspectives on things
based on their own experiences. It is helpful to learn how
others see the world, because it will help you see it clearer!

2 **Always try to do right, even in the wrong circumstances.**
Oprah had a hard childhood because of her strained
relationship with her mother, whom she was sent to live with
when Hattie Mae got sick. But she always tried to be her best.

3 **Work on your craft.** No one wakes up in the morning and
becomes "the best" at what they do with no time, effort, or
practice. When Oprah was younger, she realized her favorite
things all involved language arts: Reading, writing, and public
speaking. So she worked on making herself better at all of
those things. She read books, she wrote stories, and she
even entered a public speaking competition (and won!).
All of this work led her to her future. It paid off.

4 **Just because no one else has done it before, doesn't mean
you can't be the first.** Oprah was the first black news anchor
in Baltimore. That's huge. That means that before Oprah,
there was no representation of people who looked like her
in the TV news space. Oprah knew that didn't mean there
wasn't a place for her, but she also knew it meant she'd have to
work doubly hard to break that ceiling. We're glad she did!

5 **Don't give up!** Life is not easy. Oprah knows this from her time working at the news station. People were mean to her because of the color of her skin and her name. Some people tried to sabotage her career and run her out the door by giving her roles she was too senior for. Oprah stood tall and proud and kept her eyes on her goals.

6 **It's okay to step out of your comfort zone.** Oprah was getting comfortable in Baltimore and almost didn't apply for the *A.M. Chicago* job that led to her own television show. It's nice to feel secure but growth is necessary!

7 **Don't be afraid to be silly. People love silly!** Being successful doesn't mean being serious all of the time. Remember Oprah's first show when she told the audience she had hives under her armpits? The audience loved that! Don't be afraid to show your personality in your work. It may even help you make friends.

8 **Stay humble, and remember who helped you along the way.** When you become really successful, it's easy to forget the people who helped you get to that place. It's important to credit those who came before you. Oprah keeps a photo of her grandmother on her desk, and always remembers to thank those who took chances on her early in her career. She never got too big for her britches.

9 **Do with intention.** Always ask yourself why you're doing something. Is it helping someone else? Is it making the world better? Is it adding to your goals? Oprah always set her intentions to make her work meaningful. You can do the same!

10 **Give back!** Oprah gives back in ways big and small. You don't have to be a millionaire (or a billionaire) to make a difference for someone in need. Start now!

Grab a sheet of paper & a pencil and answer these questions!

Oprah made her mark talking to lots of different people.
If you had your own TV show and could invite three people
to come and talk to you, who would you choose?
Why would you choose those people?

What kinds of questions do you like to ask and answer?
What kinds of questions do you not like to ask and answer?
Why or why not?

Oprah said she wanted to be paid to do something.
Do you remember what that one thing was?
What would you like to be paid to do?
What do you think that means?

Imagine you could have your own talk show.
What would your talk show be called?
Would it have a theme song?
Who would sing it?

Further reading

Check out these other great resources by Oprah, her mentor Dr. Maya Angelou, and her best friend Gayle King! We've also included books in the spirit of Oprah and her life.

Non-fiction
What I Know for Sure by Oprah Winfrey
The Wisdom of Sundays by Oprah Winfrey
Words That Matter by The Oprah Magazine
Note to Self by Gayle King
I Know a Woman by Kate Hodges and Sarah Papworth
Young, Gifted and Black by Jamia Wilson and Andrea Pippins
The Gutsy Girl by Caroline Paul
Rebel Voices by Louise Kay Stewart
Success Principles for Teens by Jack Canfield and Kent Healy
I Am That Girl by Alexis Jones
Rad American Women by Kate Schatz and Miriam Klein Stahl

Poetry
And Still I Rise by Dr. Maya Angelou

Advanced reading (parental guidance advised)
I Know Why the Caged Bird Sings by Dr. Maya Angelou
Letter to My Daughter by Dr. Maya Angelou
The Bluest Eye by Toni Morrison
The Color Purple by Alice Walker
Little Black Book by Otegha Uwagba

Websites
O Magazine online

To Ari, Oprah's biggest fan, and who will one day run for President and win—C.M.

Brimming with creative inspiration, how-to projects, and useful information to enrich your everyday life, Quarto Knows is a favourite destination for those pursuing their interests and passions. Visit our site and dig deeper with our books into your area of interest: Quarto Creates, Quarto Cooks, Quarto Homes, Quarto Lives, Quarto Drives, Quarto Explores, Quarto Gifts, or Quarto Kids.

First Published in 2019 by Frances Lincoln Children's Books, an imprint of The Quarto Group.
400 First Avenue North, Suite 400, Minneapolis, MN 55401, USA.
T (612) 344-8100 F (612) 344-8692 **www.QuartoKnows.com**

ISBN 978-1-78603-736-7

The illustrations were created in paper. Set in Brandon Grotesque and Bebas Neue.

Published by Rachel Williams. Designed by Sinem Erkas.
Paper Modelling by Sinem Erkas and Christopher Noulton.
Paper assistance by Tijen Erkas.
Edited by Katy Flint. Production by Jenny Cundill.

Manufactured in China 122018
9 8 7 6 5 4 3 2 1

Photo credits p14: A young Oprah Winfrey from her high school yearbook at East Nashville High School in Tennessee, 1971 © REX/Shutterstock; p16: Oprah Winfrey wins Miss Fire Prevention title in her hometown of Nashville, 1971 © REX/Shutterstock; p50: Oprah Winfrey's Leadership Academy Construction, 2006 © Per-Anders Pettersson via Getty Images; p54: Actress and TV talk show host Oprah Winfrey poses with the Cecil B. DeMille Award, 2018 © FREDERIC J. BROWN via Getty Images.